Aboard
Pacific Princess

The Princess Cruises Love Boat

PAUL CURTIS

2nd Edition

By the Same Author

High Tea on the Cunard Queens

The Oasis Sisters – The World's Biggest Cruise Ships

A History of Professional Photography in Australia

Copyright © 2019 Paul Curtis

ABOARD PACIFIC PRINCESS
The Princess Cruises Love Boat

2nd edition

www.paulcurtis.com.au

Cover image: © Princess Cruises

First published as *The Pacific Princess- The New Love Boat* in 2005 by Rose Publishing Co. (Copyright 2005)

All rights reserved. Without limiting the rights under copyright above, no part of this publication may be produced, stored or introduced into a retrieval system, or transmitted in any form or by any means (electronic, mechanical, photocopying, recording or otherwise without the prior written permission of both the copyright owner and the publisher.

Design: Stergiou Books Limited

ISBN: 978-0-9757266-6-2

Contents

CHAPTER 1
The Love Boat 9

CHAPTER 2
Transforming a R3 into a Princess 17

CHAPTER 3
Designing and Building 27

CHAPTER 4
About Ship. 43

CHAPTER 5
A Carnival of Cruising 55

CHAPTER 6
Food, Glorious Food 75

CHAPTER 7
Ports of Call 85

CHAPTER 8
Pieces of Eight. 91

CHAPTER 9
The Princess Fleet Round-Up 101

CHAPTER I

The Love Boat

Some cruise ships are longer than the Eiffel Tower is tall; others are so wide that if they attempted to enter the Panama Canal they would stick faster than Big Ben attempting to pass through the eye of a needle; a few travel at such speeds that the wind makes it impossible to stand upright on an open deck; while others surround you with such luxury that you have to hock your entire life savings to even dream of a single night aboard.

The *Pacific Princess* is none of these. Thank heavens! But she can still lay claim to representing two major changes in the history of cruising. Not bad for a ship that first ventured the seas as recently as 1999. But such is the lady's inheritance.

The first factor is the fleet history of sailing under first the P&O and now the Princess Cruises flag. As such, the *Pacific Princess* is now a key member of Carnival Cruise Lines, the world's major shipping conglomerate.

The founder of the giant Carnival Corporation, Ted Arison, revolutionised cruising by removing it from the exclusive preserve of the rich and famous by setting cruise prices within the reach of all. Ted is considered the father of the

modern cruise ship business. Without Ted's business acumen, energy and drive, the cruise industry could have gone the way of a steam-driven dodo to cassettes, CDs and ladies whig shops.

The second factor is the sheer show business magic of her name. As the star of the top rating *The Love Boat* television series, the original *Pacific Princess* made that ship name the most talked about since the *Titanic*. When the new ship replaced the original ship, she immediately took on all the glory of her namesake.

The great thing about the filming of all those high jinks aboard *The Love Boat* was that it totally changed people's perception of cruise ship holidays. Previously, most people thought cruising was for those who were not only rich and elderly but, worse still, just plain boring. Well, nine series of top rating television shows certainly changed all that! After seeing all the fun and mayhem that the show's 'passengers' were getting up to on their cruises, viewers besieged travel agents in their thousands. Even if, up until the first screening of *The Love Boat*, passengers had been inclined to be a trifle sedate, they certainly abandoned all of that after they had seen the program.

So you see why the *Pacific Princess* is such a significant ship, even although she was not the same as that used in the television series. After all, our *Pacific Princess* was not even a sparkle in her designer's eye when, in 1975, television producer Aaron Spelling approached Princess Cruises about filming a new television show at sea.

At first, the company officials did not exactly leap around with joy at the thought of having a television film company trailing cables all over one of their beautiful cruise ships. And indeed, when it was learned that Spelling said he merely wanted to shoot a 'pilot', there was great consternation. Princess Cruises' officials tended to the view that pilots were not only perfectly harmless individuals, but rather good at getting their ships in and out of a port's shallow waters. However, once that confusion had been overcome and seeing the publicity that could flow, Spelling was allowed to shoot his television pilot aboard the Sun Princess. The networks not only liked it, they wanted a complete series. Having crossed this hurdle, it was decided to use the newly acquired and larger *Pacific Princess* for the filming. The first episode went to air in 1977 and proved an instant ratings success. It became one of the world's most watched television shows. The nine-season series went on and on and then, just when you thought it was finally finished, the repeats started! Aboard the real *Pacific Princess*, business boomed, and the frequently televised berths could not be filled fast enough.

This first *Pacific Princess* also went under a stage name. She was built as the *Sea Venture* in 1971 for Flagship Cruises. At just over 20,000 gross registered tons, she was quite considerably smaller than our *Pacific Princess* and by no means as comfortable or as good looking.

During one of shipping's occasional corporate shuffles, Princess Cruises had purchased the *Sea Venture* in 1975. Princess Cruises was itself changed from Norwegian ownership to that of the British-based P&O Cruises. At that time, there was certainly a need to do some very substantial shuffling indeed. P&O had one of the world's most famous fleets of traditional ocean liners making passages around the world, but the combined assault of ballooning oil prices and the introduction of the jumbo jet was wreaking havoc. Shipping company profits rapidly dwindled as passengers forsook their breezy, morning strolls around spacious promenade decks and opted to sardine themselves into the uncomfortable, narrow confines of the jumbos.

For passenger ships to survive it meant shifting focus from passage making to cruising and P&O firmly set its sights on the American cruise market. The popularity of the television series could not have come at a better time and the first *Pacific Princess* was soon established as the star of all cruise ships.

But no matter how many Oscars and facelifts a famous actress might have, inevitably the time comes to cast for new talent. After 27 years of service, P&O announced that the old *Pacific Princess* would be retired from the prestigious Princess fleet. For Princess Cruises, the quest had begun for a new Love Boat: bigger, modern and even more luxurious.

The search ended in an unlikely place—Papeete, Tahiti. There, strangled in red tape and going under the equally unlikely name of R3, was a magnificent near-new vessel. After extensive and painfully complicated negotiations, in August 2002, P&O Princess Cruises secured their replacement ship.

On 27 October 2002, the *Pacific Princess* made her final voyage under that name. She sailed from New York, crossing the Atlantic for the last time, to take on a new role in the Mediterranean. Here, her new owners, the Spanish–based Pullmantur Cruises, relinquished her crown and recast her as the Pacific.

 The *R3* was thus able to ascend the throne and become the new *Pacific Princess*. For Princess Cruises, it was a case of the Princess is dead: long live the Princess!

VITAL STATISTICS

THE FIRST PACIFIC PRINCESS

Formerly Sea Venture

Year Built: 1971

Shipyard: Rheinstahl Nordseewerke, Germany

Registry: Great Britain

Gross Registered Tonnage (GRT): 20,636 tons

Length: 553 ft

Beam: 81 ft

Draft: 24.5 ft

Passenger elevators: 4

Decks: 7

Passengers: 717

Crew: 350

Cabins: 238 outside, 67 inside

Passenger Space Ratio: 29

Engines: two diesel 13,240 kW

VITAL STATISTICS

PACIFIC PRINCESS
Formerly: Renaissance R3
Year built: 1999
Refurbished: 2002
Shipyard: Chantiers de l'Atlantique (Alstom).
Registry: Gibraltar
Gross Registered Tonnage (GRT): 30,277 tons
Length: 593 feet
Beam: 83 feet
Draft: 19.5 feet
Passenger Elevators: 4
Decks: 11
Public Decks: 9
Passengers: 684
Crew: 373
Cabins: 317 outside, 25 inside
Passenger Space Ratio: 44
Engines: two diesel-electric: 18,600 kW

In her final stages of completion the R3 painted black. As the Pacific Princess, she revels in her white splendor.

CHAPTER 2

Transforming a R3 into a Princess

The story of the R3 is quite unusual. Indeed, without the benefit of hindsight's twenty-twenty perfect vision, it all sounds most improbable. But it happened like this.

Firstly, let's look at what it takes to get into the cruise ship business. The costs are horrendous: guaranteed to max out even a multi-millionaire's credit card. For starters, building even a small ship will set you back well over a hundred million US dollars. Then you have to find about 370 highly trained officers and crew to staff it. Next you have to maintain and run it. Just stopping by to top up the tanks can see the fuel pump hit 750,000 litres.

Even then, you are not ready to open for businesses. You have to launch a major sales and advertising campaign to find about 650 people to fill up all those berths for each and every week of the year. By now you have raised sufficient funds to clear the bank debt of an entire impoverished South American country. And you have not even left port!

At every opportunity in port, the paint crew is over the side to give the lady's paint a touch-up.

Against this, you have to consider that if you had invested all that money in a fine hotel, you would have secured century-lasting good old bricks and mortar on land that is yours for all eternity. The cruise ship, on the other hand, has an average lifetime of a little more than 30 years. After that it is off the scrap yards where all you end up with is a big stack of razor blades. Considering the size of the investment, you certainly do not have much time to get your money back, let alone show a profit.

So, the cruise business is not for the faint-hearted. The miracle is that anyone even considers it at all. But such is the imagination, or the folly, of human beings.

And it is a very competitive business as well, both with other cruise lines and the airlines. Now into this scenario comes the company that was to eventually commission the building of the Pacific Princess. Arriving on the scene in the late 1980s, Renaissance Cruises were relative newcomers facing a chequered future. Founded by the Norwegian ship owner Fearley & Eger, Renaissance Cruises originally specialised in small, comfortable, yacht-like cruise ships of around 2,800 gross registered tons. Even at this early stage they demonstrated an unwillingness to get bogged down in the mental machinations of coming up with imaginative names for their ships. They contented themselves with simply numbering their vessels from *Renaissance I* through to *Renaissance VIII*.

With a ship building program of US$200 million, the company was financially stretched. Then came the Gulf War and bookings plummeted by seventy-five per cent.

This was the *coup de grâce* for the Norwegians and in September 1991, Fearley & Eger filed for bankruptcy. It was one of the largest collapses in Norway's history. However, Renaissance itself was saved from closure after a joint take-over by the Italian Cameli Group and the US tour company Luxury Cruises, which was controlled by Edward

One of the advantages of a smaller ship is that they can dock in more places. Here we see Pacific Princess sneaking below Sydney Harbour Bridge into the inner harbour.

Rudner, who purchased the fleet for US$13 million and assumed the debt.

Far from retiring to lick their wounds, the new management decided that, to run a profitable operation, they needed bigger ships! And not just one: they wanted two! All this was taking place at a time when the world cruise industry was being plagued by the political fall out of the explosion of a TWA aircraft and the bomb at the Atlanta Olympics.

You can imagine the negotiations with the shipbuilders and governments, but finally they succeeded in getting the giant French shipbuilding yard, Chantiers de l'Atlantique, and the French Government, to come to the party. Next, they commissioned one of the world's most respected design companies, John McNeece of London, to come up with a design that had the intimate and tasteful style of a stately English country home.

When the owners saw their first ship, they were so delighted with the look of the ship they flipped and almost immediately decided that it wasn't two such ships they wanted. What they really needed was eight! And to the delight of the designers at John McNeece, they were all to look exactly the same.

And so, the R series was born: eight near-identical ships, each costing US$185 million in one of the most remarkable deals in shipbuilding history. To achieve this, further financial support and loan guarantees came from the French-based industrial giant Alstom, which included Chantiers de l'Atlantique in its shareholdings. It became the second largest order in the cruise ship construction history being only surpassed by Carnival's Fantasy class.

But then things stared to get even more unusual. With ships popping like peas out of a pod from Chantiers, Renaissance decided that coming up with individual names was far too difficult. Instead, none too romantically, they called them *R1*, *R2*, *R3* and so on up to *R8*.

Cruise ship owners like ships to be instantly recognisable and to this end Princess Cruises repainted the bows of all their ships with their large 'sea witch' logo.

The *R1* entered service in July 1999 and was the first cruise ship to ban passengers from smoking. Operating out of Piraeus, the *R1* cruised the Aegean and the west Mediterranean along with sister ship *R2*.

The date of the keel laying for the *R3* was 19 December 1997. She was delivered in July 1999 and, as promised when Renaissance negotiated its building loan program with the French Government, she was sent to operate out of Tahiti and cruise French Polynesia. *R4* joined her at Papeete three months later.

The series was completed in 2001 with the launch of the *R8*. She primarily served in the Baltic while *R5*, *R6* and *R7* covered varying areas of the Mediterranean.

Aboard *R3*, as with all Renaissance ships a strict non-smoking policy was enforced. This was commendable, but, at the time, very brave, particularly when it is considered that both Americans and the French had national tendencies to smoke like chimneys.

And if that was not heroic enough, Renaissance made it clear that children were not welcome. Renaissance also suffered a difficult relationship with its travel agents. Renaissance decided to solve these problems by dispensing with travel agencies altogether. But the new policy of going for direct marketing and promoting itself on the web only led to declining revenues.

Losses reportedly reached US$95 million on revenues of US$580 million. In 2001, a UK investment firm put in $85 million in equity and restructured US$220 million of debt. Then a new management team announced that it would think up some real names for the fleet. It also attempted to woo the travel agents again, but by this time most of them were well and truly miffed.

The problems of attracting passengers intensified amongst muttered murmurings of financial instability. These turned into a deafening roar in the wake of the September 11 terrorist attacks. Just on two weeks later, 25 September 2001, the inevitable happened and Renaissance filed for Chapter 11 protection in the US Bankruptcy Court for the Southern District of Florida,

Imagine having your bags packed, your aeroplane ticket in hand and a taxi tooting outside your front door when you get a call from a friend to say that you had better check the Renaissance website. this is the notice that was posted to There a notice was posted which said:

> *Renaissance Cruises has ceased all cruise operations. Passengers and crew currently onboard our vessels are being disembarked and travel arrangements are being made to get them safely home. Customers with upcoming bookings should contact their credit card companies or travel agents for refund arrangements. Information about our bankruptcy case will be available on this web site soon. We apologise for any inconvenience you will experience and thank you for your prior support of Renaissance Cruises.*

On 26 September 2001, *R3* and *R4* were seized by creditors and laid up in Papeete. By October, the remainder of the Renaissance fleet was laid up originally at Gibraltar and then moved to Marseilles in the south of France

Although in late 2002 former Renaissance Chief Executive Officer Frank Del Rio formed a new partnership called Oceana Cruises and leased two of the former R ships, to all intents and purposes, the Renaissance was over.

In August 2002, P&O Princess Cruises moved to the rescue and announced the acquisition of both *R3* and *R4* through a lease purchase structure agreement. In essence, the deal was that P&O Princess would lease the two ships for approximately two years from the fourth quarter of 2002. At the end of the lease period, the company would purchase the two ships at a fixed price of around US$150 million.

Under the terms of the acquisition contracts, the two vessels were to be deployed in the Pacific for the first two years of their operation by P&O Princess.

R4 was at last mercifully renamed the *Tahitian Princess* and her home port was nominated as Papeete, Tahiti for a further three years. The R3 was selected as the new Love Boat and duly named Pacific Princess.

The Pacific Princess was put on a split deployment divided between Princess Cruises in the United States and P&O Cruises in Australia. For six months of the year she would be part of the Princess fleet and offer itineraries throughout French Polynesia and other parts of the Pacific region. For the other half of the year the ship's home port would be Sydney, where she would offer premium cruises to Australians under the P&O Cruises Australia brand. Her main destinations would be French New Caledonia and elsewhere in the South Pacific. Peter Ratcliffe, chief executive of P&O Princess Cruises, explained that the *Pacific Princess* would operate for half of the year under the Princess brand and for the other half of the year under the P&O Cruises Australia brand. This would enable the company to operate in the peak summer period year-round, selling across the northern and the southern hemispheres.

Even at this stage, it was not time for P&O Princess Cruises to put away their cheque book. The *R3*'s black painted hull had to be transformed to the line's all white livery. Modifications were also made to improve the space usage of deck ten's forward-facing Pacific Lounge. Previously this had been used as a clubby sports bar complete with television sets and only a small dance floor. Princess Cruises transformed it into a 190-seat nightclub with a tropical setting and enlarged the dance floor.

Once this was completed, she emerged shining white and sporting Princess Cruises familiar 'sea witch' logo on her funnel. Only then was she ready to sail as the new *Pacific Princess*.

The ship's library features a fireplace and a tromp l'oeil ceiling.

CHAPTER 3

Designing and Building

High up on the Pacific Princess's tenth deck is the most beautiful library you could ever hope to find afloat. Beneath pastel painted, domed, trompe l'oeil ceilings and within walls lined with mahogany book cabinets, you can settle snugly into the plush leather of comfortably cushioned chesterfields and relax with a good read. It is the book lover's perfect haven for peace and tranquillity. And if you glance up from your reading, look through the wide windows over the decks to the broad vista of a blue ocean and happen to catch a glimpse of a palm-fringed coral atoll slowly drifting across a sizzling sun setting into a silver sea: well, even the most cynical of jaded hearts could be forgiven for skipping the odd beat or two. You really have to pinch yourself: just to check if it is all real.

Ouch! It is real, but how did it come to be real? What is it about this room, this deck, this ship, this place? After all, in an inventory of fact, you are really only surrounded by an assemblage of raw materials such as leather, wood, fabric and steel: all welded, twisted and melded together. So how do you go about imbuing this material mish-mash with

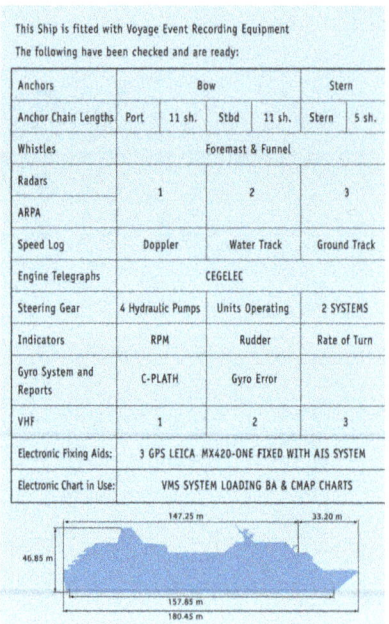

Navigational vital statistics at a glance – a copy of the guide given to a port pilot when boarding the ship.

all the atmosphere and feel of a regency home set deep in the English countryside?

On a cold January day, over a pint of bitter in a typical old London pub, only three minutes walk from the Islington tube station, I put this question to Ron Hughes, the project leader of the John McNeece team that designed the Pacific Princess. From the somewhat prosaic offices around the corner, the John McNeece company's inspirational approach has led to it becoming one of the most respected names in international design. Its credits include total designs and redesigns for such ships as *The QE2, Oriana, Auroroa, The World of Residensea, the Sovereign of the Seas and the Black Watch*. The company is also famous for its work in hotel and corporate office design.

Ron Hughes, project leader for the McNeece Pacific Princess design team.

Ron, an associate director and head of the Travel and Leisure division, explains that it was a mammoth task and that McNeece spent six years on the R series ships. In the years between 1997 and 2000, no fewer than eight of these vessels were completed at Alstom's Chantiers de l'Atlantique's Saint-Nazaire shipyard on the French channel coast.

The design team mostly totalled fifteen, which included six designers, plus three or four experts working on furniture, fittings and equipment, and another three or four on graphics. Because the owners loved the look and atmosphere of the first ship, all of the eight ships are almost identical in appearance and interior design. There are just a few tweaks between the various vessels.

Pennie Nicholl, head of interior decoration at McNeece, was responsible for the soft furnishings side of the job. This covered everything from the weave, colour and pattern of carpets, curtains and furniture right though to commissioning all of the artwork that hangs aboard the ship. Then there was the sourcing of the thousands of accessories, ornaments and antiques. Penny spent years practically living in the shipbuilder's yard and running her own team of French contractors

Ron Hughes explained that with modern shipbuilding methods, the traditional marine architect's role has become more one of cooperation between the shipbuilding yard and the quantity surveyor, and that it is the design team that gives the ship its character and personality. There is no doubt that while many once famous shipyards have lagged behind due to a combination of poor government support and the ability to cope with change, Alstom's Chantiers de l'Atlantique yard has built itself into one of the most prestigious names in shipbuilding in the world.

Launching from St Nazaire the old way. The France glides down the slip to the roar of drag chains and enthusiastic French citizenry. This risky procedure has now been changed for the safe and gentle flooding of a dry construction dock. Note the fine bow, which is the traditional hallmark of a transatlantic liner. This differs greatly from cruise ship, such as the Pacific Princess, which do not have to be built to cut through the huge waves that mark the perils of the North Atlantic winter.

Over the last few decades, shipbuilding has gone through more changes than a chameleon at a Saturday night disco. Traditionally, ships were built on slips — a shore-based, long cradle that was first heavily greased. Onto this the keel would be laid and then the hull would be assembled onto the keel. On completion, with due pomp and ceremony and the smashing of a bottle of champagne across the bows for good luck, the cradle bearing the ship would be released so that she could begin her perilous descent along the sloping ways into the water. Heavy drag chains attached to the cradle were used to check the ship's ever-increasing speed. The launch would be accompanied by the deafening roar of thousands of metres of heavy drag chains, clouds of rising dust and cheers from workers and official visitors. The risk of disaster was enormous. Could she be stopped before she hit the bank on the other side of the river? Would she float, heavily list or even topple over? No wonder crowds of more than a hundred thousand used to flock to river banks to watch the launchings of the big ships with such interest.

Over the years, the much easier dry-docking process of construction has been adopted. Thus, the launch of a ship today is a relatively casual affair. The nail–biting suspense, the hammering free of wedges holding back thousands of tons of steel on a sloping slip, the thundering of desperately struggling drag chains and the clouds of dust have all been replaced by the gentle gurgle of water flooding into an enclosed basin to allow the imprisoned vessel to be simply floated free.

But that does not mean to say that the boys at Chantiers de l'Atlantique do not know how to put on a good launch party. Every one of the many ships the yard completes each year, are sent off with a dramatic firework display and party to which all the ship's workers and their families are invited.

And this is no rare event. Between 2000 and 2003, almost one third of the world's orders for cruise ships were awarded to Chantiers. The company delivered four cruise ships in 2000 and six in 2001. Chantiers also won the prestigious order to build the world's then biggest ship, the transat-

The Pacific Princess naming ceremony was held in Sydney's famous Darling Harbour on the 8th December 2002. Officiating were the ship's Godmother, Gabi Hollows and Captain Christopher Rynd. Gabi is a highly respected Australian who worked with her husband in remote communities to prevent blindness amongst Australian Aboriginal people.

lantic liner Queen Mary 2. She was delivered on schedule in December 2003.

For almost 150 years, virtually the entire township of Saint-Nazaire has been living the human, industrial and technical adventure of shipbuilding. Saint-Nazaire is a city of prestigious ocean liners. It has been the birthplace of giants of the seas which have become legends in their own rights. These include the classic transatlantic liner Normandy, completed in 1932, and the last century's longest liner, the France, which was completed in 1962. The Chantiers yard is widely recognised as having produced ships which have written new chapters in the annals of ship building.

The industrial site of the shipyard is very extensive and covers over 120 hectares along the river Loire. The site roams from steel plate storage areas to outfitting basins and can be toured by interested members of the public to gain a fascinating insight into the whole process of shipbuilding. Here you can see all the building steps, from the preparation of raw materials through to the finished ship, The company employs about five thousand men and women, all busy building everything in the way of shipping: from cruise liners, to tankers, ferries and even to military vessels.

While ship yards failed in Scotland and Ireland, the French government support ensured that Chantiers was always at the very cutting edge of the latest technology in ship building. While skills were lost in other yards around the world, they were honed and perfected at Saint-Nazaire.

Until the middle of the 20th century, ships were assembled steel plate by steel plate, from scaffoldings rising at the same rate. In the process, each steel plate is assembled to its neighbouring plate by means of rivets: big bolts brought to a white heat and then punched through the steel to join the plates together. To complete a ship the size of the famous

Normandie, Chantiers de l'Atlantique used eleven million such rivets. It was a difficult, sweaty and even dangerous task performed by only the toughest of steel workers.

In those days, on their first cruises, gullible young lady passengers were apt to be pursued by ardent ship's officers with less than honourable intentions. Such officer used to maintain, with an authoritative air that, after such a long and intense building process, the final rivet driven through the hull was made of pure gold. And as luck would have it, that final golden rivet happened to be located in their cabin. Of course!

Thus, while the replacement of riveting by the process of welding caused a dramatic improvement in the process of shipbuilding; many a ship's officer rued the loss of the opportunity to show the golden rivet. Aboard the Pacific Princess, there is not one rivet. So, ladies, don't let anybody tell you anything otherwise!

The secret of Chantiers de l'Atlantique's success has been the introduction of the block building approach. Various parts of the ship are built in separate blocks, which only when near completion are brought together to form the ship's structure.

This was the process used to build the Pacific Princess. Indeed, the same process was used by Chantiers to build the Queen Mary 2. That ship is five times bigger than the Princess, weighing in at 153,000 tons and representing 8 million working hours. Altogether, no less than 94 blocks, some of them weighing over 600 tons were needed to build

The change from riveting to welding greatly speeded up the process of ship construction.

the hull. It took 300,000 steel pieces and some 1,500 kilometres of welding to built the monster ship.

In the middle of the 1990s, in order to optimise production, Chantiers adopted a new organisation, centred on six departments. With a work force of more than 5000, the aim was to get a tighter grip on costs, delivery time and quality. In case you can't get to the Chantiers de l'Atlantique shipyard, here is a brief tour of the ship building process that went into the Pacific Princess.

Step 1: Reception of the Steel Plates

This is where it all begins. A ship is above all an assembly of steel plates of all kinds of size and resistance. Their thickness varies between 4 mm and 20 mm.

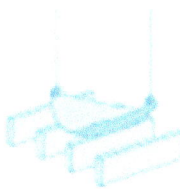

Step 2: Prefabrication and Forming

In the plasma cutting workshop, the steel plates are cut along patterns corresponding to the different pieces of the hull. Seventy steel plates, representing up to 1500 different pieces, can be cut each day. As an example, the hull of the cruise ship Millennium, (90 228 tons) delivered in June 2000, contained 180,000 pieces

Step 3: Making the Panels

The steel plates are then welded together in the prefabrication workshops, thus constituting the panels. The huge, flat panels workshop is extremely sophisticated and considered the most modern of its kind in the world. The steel panels created here can measure up to 32 metres.

Step 4: Pre-outfitting

At this stage, part of the networks for electricity, water and piping are being installed so the block can become a complete unit.

Step 5. Block Construction

The blocks are then taken to the pre-assembly area before being welded together until they form whole parts of the ship. It's all rather like a giant game of Leggo.

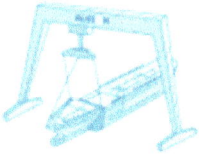
Step 6. Assembly of the blocks

These parts are then assembled in the huge construction dock. The ship begins to take shape.

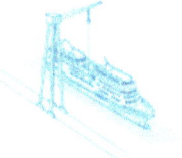
Step 7. Outfitting

The ship now has her definite silhouette. The last stage, that is the outfitting, finishes all that is left to be installed on board.

Step 8. Sea Trials

Once she has been finished and declared fit for service, the ship can start her career.

Step 9. Delivery

The moment of celebration, a completed cruise ship ready to sail the seas.

The following table is a copy of the original check list used by McNeece in the building of the Pacific Princess.

ITEM	DESCRIPTION	SUPPLIER
DECK 5		
MAIN RESTAURANT & PRE-DINNER BAR		
Ceiling Tromp l'oeil	Acrylic paints	Paul Treasure, Hampshire, UK
Wall finish	Burr Walnut panels with period style mouldings	SMAT, France
Floor finish	80/20, wool/nylon Axminster broadloom carpet to special design by McNeece	Ulster Carpets, Nthn Ireland
	Rosso Levano marble around bar and waiter stations	
Cabinet work	Walnut	
Mirror panels	Antique bronzed	
DECK 10		
LIBRARY		
Ceiling Trompe l'oeil	Acrylic paints	Paul Treasure, Hampshire, UK
Wall finish	Mahogany panels with period style mouldings	ERBOS, France
Floor finish	80/20, wool/nylon Axminster broadloom carpet to special design by McNeece	Ulster Carpets, Nthn Ireland
Cabinet work	Mahogany	
Mirror panels	Antique bronzed	
Fireplace	Botticino marble	

DECK 10		
OBSERVATION LOUNGE / SPORTS BAR		
Wall finish	Crown cut mahogany wall panelling	
Floor finish	80/20, wool/nylon Axminster broadloom carpet to special design by McNeece	Ulster Carpets, Nthn Ireland
	Polished Mahogany hardwood dance floor	
Banquette seating	Leather, deep buttoned Chesterfield-style	
Blinds	Electronic solar blinds	
Bar	Mahogany bar top with leather bar front	
DECK 5		
LOUNGE BAR / CASINO		
Wall finish	Mahogany wall panels with period style mouldings	Alpha Intl., France
Floor finish	80/20, wool/nylon Axminster broadloom carpet to special design by McNeece	Ulster Carpets, Nthn Ireland
	Rojo Alicante marble around bar with black granite insets	
Cabinet work	Mahogany	
Bar	Mahogany bar front with bronze trim and black lacquered infill. Black granite bar top	

DECK 10

AMERICAN RESTAURANT

Wall finish	Dark mahogany vertical planked panels and framing	
Floor finish	80/20, wool/nylon Axminster broadloom carpet to special design by McNeece	Ulster Carpets, Nthn Ireland
	Polished mahogany planked flooring	
Cabinet work	Mahogany	
Cornice	Period style dentiled cornice with painted timber effect	
Bar	Mahogany bar front panels with black granite bar top	

DECK 10

ITALIAN RESTAURANT

Wall finish	Venetian polished plaster effect finish	
Wall frieze panels	Moulded plaster relief panels depicting ancient Greek and Roman scenes. Venetian polished plaster effect finish	
Floor finish	80/20, wool/nylon axminster broadloom carpet to special design by McNeece	Ulster Carpets, Nthn Ireland
	Brecha tavamera and Botticino classico marble in front of bar	
Cabinet work	Lime washed timber finish	

Cornice	Period style dentiled	
Bar	Brecha tavamerela marble bar front and bar top	
Georgian balustrading	Dwarf balustrading in natural stone effect finish	
DECK 9		
MAIN RESTAURANT & OUT DOOR CAFE		
Wall finish	Tromp l'oeil panels depicting English country house scenes, with dragged paint effect framework	
Floor finish	80/20, wool/nylon Axminster broadloom carpet to special design by McNeece	Ulster Carpets, Nthn Ireland
	Brecha tavamera and Botticino classico marble in front of bar	
Cabinet work	Lime washed oak timber finish	
Cornice	Period style dentiled mouldings	
Bar	Lime washed oak timber bar front and granite bar top	
Georgian balustrading	Dwarf balustrading in natural stone effect finish	

DECK 4		
RECEPTION		
Ceiling feature	Acrylic Red and opal back lit acrylic panels within in bronze framework. Lighting effect changes in time with sun rise and sunset	
Wall finish	Mahogany panels with period style mouldings	
	Ashlar style stone effect finish to shops; with black painted framework and bronze grilles.	
Floor finish	80/20, wool/nylon Axminster broadloom carpet to special design by McNeece	Ulster Carpets, Nthn Ireland
	White Carrera marble with black marble insets and border	
Cabinet work	Mahogany	
Reception desk and Excursion counter	Alpi Verdi marble counter front and top, with mahogany cabinet work and panelled shutters	
Staircase	Laser cut scroll metal work; black painted with applied leaf details painted gold, with antique bronze handrail	

DECK 5		
CABARET LOUNGE		
Ceiling feature	Profiled plaster	
Wall finish	Crushed velvet wrapped panels with gilded period style mouldings and walnut framing	
	Gilded, embossed, hand-painted leather-wrapped panels with walnut framing, and Corinthian column features	
Floor finish	80/20, wool/nylon Axminster broadloom carpet to special design by McNeece	Ulster Carpets, Nthn Ireland
	Black granite in front of bar	
	Timber sprung dance floor with intricate inlaid timber pattern of Wenge and Maple hardwoods	
Cabinet work	Mahogany	
Bar	Mahogany bar front panels with black lacquered and bronze detailing and black granite bar top. Look carefully for medallion on bar front dedicated to famous Texan guitarist	

This table was used as the McNeece source guide. Specifications for the Sports Bar were later changed by Princess Cruises.

CHAPTER 4

About Ship

In these days of mega-ship building, the Pacific Princess is neither a super modern colossus, nor a yacht-sized ship. At just over 30,000 tons, she occupies an interesting small to middle-ground which is relatively rare. She is large enough to provide many of the services expected on upscale ships while still retaining a sense of intimacy. Her size also means she is small enough to visit many of the off the beaten track ports around the world. The Princess is, in fact, as Goldilocks would say, 'just right'.

The general air of spaciousness is considerably enhanced by the fact that passengers are not crammed in. Indeed, using the standard measuring system of space per passenger, the Pacific Princess is one of the most spacious ships in the world. She is mercifully free of the long lines for service that plague so many ships. Indeed, service all round is of a very high standard as there are 373 crew to serve a maximum capacity of 684 passengers. This means there is virtually one crew member for every two passengers.

There is a total of eleven decks and you will have plenty of opportunity for exercise as passengers have access to decks three and above. There are four elevators, but for the

energetic there are the stairwells located at the fore and aft ends of the ship. When you board the Pacific Princess from the gangway, you enter the aft deck stairwell on deck four, which has an elegant two tiered-deck foyer with a signature grand, red-carpeted, *'Titanic'* staircase. This is an ideal spot to momentarily pause in a casual but elegant pose for a photograph. Don't worry, the ship's photographers will be there!

CABIN

When first boarding, the first thing is generally a visit to the allocated cabin. And there are no problems for passengers here as they are all very comfortable. Located on decks three, four, six, seven and eight, there are 349 staterooms and suites. Of these, 92 per cent have an ocean view and 68 per cent have their own balcony. While all are well sound insulated, the cabin sizes vary. There are 27 inside cabins of 158 square feet and 76 standard outside cabins of 216 square feet. Moving up scale, there are 170 outside cabins with balconies. Now we're travelling in real style! The large number of balcony outside cabins is made possible by placing cabin decks above the public rooms rather than the older ship design concept of having the public rooms at the top.

All cabins feature: twin beds that can be converted into a queen-size bed; a spacious closet; bathroom with shower; hairdryers; private safe; multi-function phone; multi-channel music system and remote-controlled colour television. This features movies, CNN, ESPN, TNT, Discovery, and, of course, the view from the bridge camera. Some cabins are also equipped with convertible sofas and upper Pullman berths to allow for triple or quadruple occupancy for the extra friendly.

The grand staircase leads to a shopping arcade.

The ship's library is reminscent of an exclusive London private club.

There are fifty-two mini-suites which measure 322 square feet if you include the balcony. And why wouldn't you? It's the best seat in the house! The mini-suites offer the additional amenity of a sitting area with a sofa bed; the bathroom has a tub and a shower. There are terrycloth robes and a refrigerator with a mini-bar. This is bliss class.

For those who aspire ever further, there are 12 'owner suites' which add a larger private balcony; guest bathroom; a sitting area that converts for dining; a marble appointed, full bathroom with a whirlpool tub; and an entertainment centre with two televisions, CD player, receiver and three speakers. They measure between 786 and 962 square feet and are ideal for having your own parties.

PUBLIC ROOMS

Once a passenger has settled in, the next step is generally to explore the public rooms and public areas which are located on decks five, nine and ten. A good place to start is at the very top on deck 11, at the bow end of the sun deck. This offers views forward and to either side through wind-protecting, sun-glare, tinted glass screens. The forward expanse stretches the width of the ship, continuing aft on either side of a long, narrow midships deckhouse that supports the raked radio mast. A sea of turquoise Astroturf sunning space is broken up on the port side with a shuffleboard court and on the starboard side is a golf practice cage.

This deck also offers a fine view over the midships lido toward the library windows just below the base of the funnel.

The library can be reached by dropping down to deck ten and crossing aft along the one-eighth of a mile-long fitness track for joggers and walkers that overlooks the lido. So, thirteen times around that and you have notched up one nautical mile.

The entrance to the Club Restaurant.

The on-board casino gives passengers a chance to win back the cost of their cruise!

Back inside, we enter our first public interior and really there is no better place to start. This has to be one of the best rooms on any ship, any where.

The library is U-shaped with the entrance doors to port and to starboard and the wood-panelled room is richly furnished with wing-backed armchairs, chesterfields and brown leather window seats. Inside glass cabinets is a very good selection of books. Large forward and side windows, a domed frescoed skylight and a magnificent, green marble, just for show fireplace with brass surround complete an ideal hide-away for a good read.

Behind the library, to either side of the ship, you will find two speciality 90 seat restaurants: Sabatini's Italian Restaurant and The Steakhouse Stirling Grill. We will get to food later, but in the meantime if you move back along the jogging track all the way forward, you come to the nightclub, with its Polynesian-inspired décor. This was one of the few areas changed from the original R3 when it was known as the Sports Bar. The former plaid carpets and dark panelling were abandoned in favour of a more tropical look. Floor-to-ceiling windows offer great views on three sides and make for a perfect observation lounge during the day. Seating for 194 and a dance floor make it a popular evening venue.

Dropping down to deck nine we find the Lotus Spa and fitness centre. The Lotus Spa has it's own outside, private, glass-sheltered spa deck surrounded by comfortable lounge chairs. Inside is a small but embracing world of sauna and steam rooms, body wraps, facials, massage, body therapy and hair styling.

For the more energetic, on the starboard side is a fully equipped gymnasium. Again, this area features floor to ceiling glass windows and offers cardio machines and weights as well as an adjoining space for stretching and aerobics.

The spacious pool deck even offers a spa bath.

Passengers can work off any excesses at the buffet while enjoying a magnificent view from the gym.

Immediately aft of the fitness centre is a small, thirty-seat card room and a computer room equipped with eight work stations to roam the internet.

Continuing aft on deck nine, we go outside to the glass-screen sheltered midships lido area. The decks are brown and finished with a rubber compound known as Bolidt.

An open-air bar precedes a large pool flanked by two jaccuzzis and is surrounded by deck chair space. A bandstand and dance floor is in the aft amidships position. The area continues aft with more sheltered space on the port side and a barbeque kitchen on the starboard side.

These lead back inside again to the Panorama Buffet. The most popular place for lunch, this U-shaped area boasts large picture windows, seats 272 and has a pizzeria on one side and a bar on the other. A popular outside terrace dining area runs across the full width of the stern deck. Tables offer seating for two, four, six and eight people.

Deck 8 begins forward with the wheelhouse and officers' accommodation and the rest is given over to passenger staterooms. Below, on deck seven, a self-service laundry with washing machines, dryers and ironing boards, is located slightly aft of midships.

Deck six is all passenger staterooms while the whole of deck five is given over to public rooms. At the forward end we have the 350 seat Cabaret Lounge.

This is the Pacific Princess showroom and is entered on either side through a semi-circular gallery of dark wood classical columns. This room is large but manages to retain an intimate atmosphere with gold Regency chairs circle well finished wooden tables set on a rich carpet of blue and gold. At the far end are the stage and the bandstand. In front of this, a sunken circular and ornately inlaid wooden dance floor is complemented by a similarly-shaped ceiling

Calm seas and a steady hand are the essentials for a successful champagne fountain.

recess and it is surrounded by a generous seating area. To convert the lounge to a cinema, three giant electric projection screens lower from the roof.

The bar perimeter is slightly higher again and gives a good view of the stage. On the starboard side of the bar there is a control room for lighting and sound. Throughout the length of the room and on both sides, large, floor-to-ceiling picture windows provide plenty of daylight and ocean vistas.

Moving aft on deck five, we enter a tasteful casino area, something that is all too rare on modern ships. The area is quiet and devoid of flashing lights. Instead it is decorated with hanging brass ceiling lights and sconces, layered drapery, and ornate carpeting. There are the usual roulette, blackjack and slot machines, but an adjoining bar has small tables set up for chess and other board games. This cosy 60 seat lounge features wingback chairs, plush sofas, a piano and a faux fireplace to give a private club atmosphere.

The starboard side alleyway to the gaming tables features a photo gallery for the display of the pictures taken by the ship's photographers. When not in use, the gallery panels fold away to form imitation bookshelves to maintain the ship's elegant interior.

Moving further aft two shops line the midships passage to the handsome vestibule of the upper lobby with its art gallery, grand piano, recessed skylight and ornately adorned stairwell leading down to the reception area formerly known on ships at the Purser's Office. In the aft, port corner is the shore excursions office and forward of this is the ship's medical centre.

Back on deck five and aft of the grand staircase is the eighth of the Pacific Princess's bars: The Club Bar which serves as an entrance to the Club Dining Room. This intimate bar is flanked with bookcases mid-toned panelling. A white-mantled fireplace and frescoed backlit ceiling recess complete the cosy atmosphere.

The restaurant itself is cleverly broken up into intimate areas via balustrades and decorated in subdued pinks and blues. A circular Odeon-style ceiling recess features amidships, while comfortable upholstered dining chairs seat 354 passengers.

In 2017, Pacific Princess underwent a two-week multi-million-dollar renovation with the introduction in places of some new modern colours, patterns and textures while still keeping the small ship essence and traditional architecture.

The staterooms were refurbished, and new bedding installed. Dining rooms were smartened up, the Atrium and Pool Deck were modernised, and 178,000 square feet of new carpet was laid.

No matter where you wander on the Pacific Princess, in the public rooms or on the decks, there is a general feeling of spaciousness and plenty of available seats to hand. This is probably due to the large number of private balconies equipped with their own chairs.

In 2019 staterooms and suites were refurbished.

CHAPTER 5

A Carnival of Cruising

There are three company names involved with the Pacific Princess: P&O Cruises, Princess Cruises and Carnival Cruise Lines. How did this come to be? One could be forgiven for asking, 'Will the real owner of the Pacific Princess please stand-up?' But once you understand the backgrounds and histories of the companies involved the answer is quite simple.

The Peninsular and Oriental Steam Navigation Company began in 1822 with a partnership between Arthur Anderson and Brodie Willcox. Arthur was born of a poor family in the Shetlands and went on to become a clerk in the British Royal Navy. Brodie McGhie Willcox was a Londoner with a strong financial background and a dour personality who went on to become a shipbroker.

After Anderson joined his company, Willcox was quick to recognise that Anderson's entrepreneurial spirit coupled with his winning ways with customers was a real boon to the company. Together, with a few of their own small

Balcony class cabins are a firm favourite with passengers.

sailing ships, coupled with the management of steamers belonging to other companies, they built a business sailing between Britain and the area of Spain and Portugal known as the Iberian Peninsula.

In both the Portuguese civil war and the quickly following Spanish civil war of the early 1830s, the partners sided with the Royal Family of each country against the insurrections. Transport demands grew and covered everything from troop-carrying to gun-running for the Royals. By 1836, in a more stable political climate, Anderson and Willcox were able to introduce a regular steamer service to the Iberian Peninsula and commenced operating under the name Peninsular Steam Navigation Company.

With the granting of British Government mail contracts, the partners set about extending their shipping routes onto India and the Orient, with the company becoming incorporated as Peninsula and Oriental in 1840. Until the opening of the Suez Canal in 1869, the company used the overland route across Egypt before passengers went on by sea. By 1845, the company had a regular steamer service that reached Malay and China.

So, P&O stands for Peninsula and Oriental and in spite of what many people have come to think, P&O has nothing to do with the word 'posh'. That word was derived from the fact that in the early days of voyaging from Europe to the Far East, ships, of course, did not have air-conditioning. Consequently, when crossing the tropics, one side of the ship would have to bear the full brunt of a searing sun for the entire day, while the other side of the ship would be in relatively cool shadow. Passengers quickly became aware of this and started booking the shady side in each direction of travel. Naturally, enough, this practice soon attracted a price premium. To secure the shady side, travel agents making such cabin requests used to mark the bookings on

FACTS YOU WERE AFRAID TO ASK

Port of Registry	Gibraltar
Call Sign	ZDDY7
Official Number	732137
Gross Registered Tonnage	30,227
Net Tonnage	11,481
Length Overall	180.45 metres
Length between Perpendiculars	157.95 metres
Moulded Breadth	25.46 metres
Total Breadth with Bridge Wings	28.3 metres
Maximum Draught	5.965 metres
Corresponding Displacement	16146 tons
Corresponding Deadweight	3376 tons
Fuel Capacity	750 tons
Fresh Water Capacity	1200 tons
Propulsion Type	Diesel Electric
Thrusters	2 bow thrusters at 750 kW each
Propellers	2 four blade fixed pitch propellers
Rudders	2 Semi-balanced, each rudder 19.4 square metres
Stabilisers	2 Each fin 9.9 square metres

the sailings from Europe as Portside Out and Starboard Home. And thus, the word 'posh' was introduced to the English language. Very smart!

While the Royal Houses of Spain and Portugal did not necessarily think Willcox and Anderson vessels particularly posh, they were very appreciative of their war time shipping services and so granted them the right to fly their national colours: the red and gold of Spain, and the blue and white of Portugal. To this day, these are still the colours of the P&O house flag.

P&O claims to be the company that discovered the concept of cruising. In the early days, ships used to just make a passage from point A to point B. There was not much comfort and passengers making the voyages did so mostly out of sheer necessity. However, as ships improved in their reliability and companies vied with each other by upgrading comfort levels, the idea eventually dawned that life aboard a ship could, in fact, be fun!

The chief and original propagandist was essayist W.M. Thackeray, who in 1844 travelled to Malta, Greece, Constantinople, the Holy Land and Egypt in a series of P&O ship connections. In his subsequent book, From Cornhill to Grand Cairo, he recounted tales of his 'delightful Mediterranean cruise'. In his praise of a leisurely life aboard a P&O passenger ship, Thackeray was subsequently joined by such famous authors as Kipling, Forster, and Trollope. By the mid-1800s, P&O had begun to promote the concept of cruising with special voyages.

Throughout the rest of the century and well into the middle of the twentieth century, P&O continued to expand. As well as mail contracts, the Crimean War, the Indian Mutiny, the Boer War, and so on, brought considerable government trooping work. This was definitely no cruise, but the profits helped the company introduce new voyage routes

Quoits is one of a cruise ship's most popular games.

to Australia and New Zealand and across the Pacific to Canada and to the western United States. But throughout the years, P&O always maintained an interest in the cruise business and promoted special voyages aboard its then novelly white painted ships. It was thus ideally positioned when, in the late 1960s, the popularity of air travel and the soaring cost of fuel oil sounded the death knell for the passage-making ship. P&O was immediately able to develop its white-painted ships into a major cruise industry.

Of particular interest to the Pacific Princess, was the formation of an actively promoted cruise division in Australia. The first Down-Under P&O cruise took place in 1932 when Strathaird sailed from Sydney on a Christmas cruise to Norfolk Island with a full complement of passengers. By 2002, P&O were the largest operator of year-round cruises from Australia and was carrying more than 60,000 Australians and New Zealanders on South Pacific cruises every year.

On the American front, in 1974, P&O acquired the US-based Princess Cruises.

Princess Cruises

This company was founded by Stanley Mc Donald with just one ship in 1964: a veteran steam ship named Princess Patricia that operated along the West coast of America. More ships followed: the Princess Italia and in 1968, the Princess Carla. After purchasing Princess Cruises, P&O brought their own Spirit of London into the company and renamed her *Sun Princess*. But the real star of the fleet in the 1970's was undoubtedly the original Pacific Princess used for filming the hit television show Love Boat.

In 1988, P&O Princess Cruises itself took over of the rival company Sitmar Cruises. This was followed with the acquisition of Aida Cruises in 1999. By the end of that year,

Golf and table tennis are popular pastimes during days at sea.

the company had 18,000 employees worldwide and carried over 700,000 passengers annually. The complement of 18 ships offered 25,600 berths.

Carnival

A comparatively recent arrival on the world shipping stage, Carnival Cruises had a humble beginning in 1972 with just one ship. By 2006 it had a fleet of around 60 vessels. By 2019 Carnival had acquired ten cruise companies and more than one hundred ships.

This phenomenal growth was brought about by the drive and commitment of Ted Arison. By adjusting traditional cost policies, Ted is credited with taking the cruise ship holiday from being the exclusive preserve of the rich to being within the reach of nearly everyone.

Ted Arison was born in 1924, studied engineering in Beirut at the American University and fought first in World War 11 and again in 1948 during the creation of Israel. Ted's father owned the Israeli ships and shipping company, M. Dizengoff & Co. Ted took over the business when his father died just after World War 11. But the company was not his key passion and in the 1950s he sold out to move into other business ventures in the United States of America.

Ted Arison's mind was more set on retirement when he teamed up with Norwegian shipping magnate Knut Kloster. Together they formed Norwegian Caribbean Lines by basing a new cruise ship, the Sunward, in Miami. The idea was to fly passenger south from the key American cities in the north rather than starting from the traditional port of New York City. This way, passengers were spared the first three cold days at sea experienced during the North American winter. The idea proved very popular and was the birth of the fly/cruise concept.

Pacific Islanders entertain passengers ashore.

Ted Arison and Knut Kloster parted company in 1972 and Ted teamed up with Meshulam Riklis of American International Travel Service to form Carnival Cruises by transforming the aging Empress of Canada into the Mardi Gras. It was not an auspicious start, as just into the inaugural sailing, the ship ran aground on a sand bar outside the port of Miami with around 300 journalists onboard! And the initial financial going was very tough indeed. But Ted was very determined in his views on how the Miami venture should be run and bought the company outright in 1974.

In 1975 he bought a second ship, the Empress of Britain and his conviction and willingness to gamble on the strength of his own ideas paid dividends. Ship followed ship and, after becoming a publicly listed company in 1987, he began to look at buying whole shipping companies as well. He purchased Holland America Line-Westours and Windstar in 1989.

In 1990, Ted passed the management reigns to his son Micky and returned to Israel to grow a new empire in technology, banking and real estate. After battling cancer, he died of a heart attack at his Tel Aviv home in 1999.

Micky certainly proved he was his father's son as he built boldly and decisively on Carnival's foundations and began a period of expansion by acquiring rival cruise companies.

At first, the acquisition of each line was viewed with concern by some in the industry. The major fear was that the ships would become alike and all would be run the same way. But Micky Arison passionately believed in preserving the brand identity of the different ships and lines. And, even with an over 40 percent share of the cruise market, the potential to increase prices was not under consideration as Arison saw the cruise dollar as being under intense competition from other sectors of the vacation industry.

Arison's battles to grow the Carnival empire has led to head on confrontations on both sides of the Atlantic with government regulators fearful of a monopoly. But Arison has successfully defended his company's growth by continually pointing out that cruising is only a tiny part of the overall holiday market.

Furthermore, his management of the lines has proved to be to the benefit of all. The crowning pinnacle of Arison's contribution to shipping is the building of the Queen Mary 2. Entering service for Cunard in January 2004, the 150,000-ton Queen Mary 2 is both the largest and, at $US800 million, the most expensive liner (not a cruise ship) ever built.

The success of Arison's business approach is best measured by the fact that in 2002, at the time that Pacific Princess's original owners were filing for bankruptcy, the Carnival Cruises' fleet was running at 97.7 per cent occupancy.

But in the turmoil that followed the infamous September 11 attacks, some shipping companies got nervous, while others believed demand would increase due to the greater security of cruise travel. This led to a period of takeovers and consolidation with Carnival Corporation and Royal Caribbean cruise lines both keen to expand. In 2002, the two companies competed to woo P&O Princess Cruises with take over offers. This led to investigations by the trade commission in both the United States and the European Union. Eventually, the regulators on both side of the Atlantic voted to allow both the Carnival and Royal Caribbean bids for P&O Princess Cruises to proceed.

By early 2003, Carnival had met P&O's condition of a dual listing of its shares in both New York and London thus giving Carnival 74% of the resulting company. Under a dual-listed merger, the two companies agreed to be run as one under a unified management, though no shares or

cash would swap hands. P&O and Carnival were to retain their separate listings.

At the time, the deal created the world's largest cruise vacation group with a total of 65 cruise ships offering approximately 100,000 lower berths, carrying 4.7 million passengers a year and operating with total assets of over US$20.0 billion. On order, for delivery over the next three years, was an additional 18 cruise ships to add approximately another 42,000 berths.

Carnival Corporation's portfolio of 13 cruise brands in North America, Europe and Australia, then comprised: Carnival Cruise Lines, Princess Cruises, Holland America Line, Costa Cruises, P&O Cruises, Cunard Line, Windstar Cruises, Seabourn Cruise Line, Ocean Village, Swan Hellenic, AIDA, A'ROSA, and P&O Cruises Australia.

NAMING CEREMONY

Some people marry twice. Pacific Princess was named twice. First there was an R3 christening ceremony on 30 August 1999 by the First Lady of Tahiti, Mrs. Tonita Flosse. Then the Pacific Princess became the first P&O Princess cruise ship to be named in Australia. The ceremony was performed at Sydney's famous Darling Harbour on Sunday 8 December 2002. For the event, the ship appointed Gabi Hollows, a popular and much respected Australian, and one of Australia's 100 Living National Treasures, as the Ship's Godmother.

Gabi originated from Gosford on the New South Wales Central Coast of Australia and was the wife of the late philanthropic eye surgeon, Fred Hollows. Gabi is the founding director of The Fred Hollows Foundation.

Gabi met Fred Hollows during her training as an orthoepist. Later, sponsored by the Royal Australian College of Ophthalmologists and the Australian Government, Gabi and Fred worked in remote areas to prevent blindness amongst Australian Aboriginal people. The news of the success of their pioneering work soon spread and they extended their work to help needy people overseas.

Gabi and Fred were married in 1980 and had five children. Sadly, Fred Hollows passed away in 1993. Since that time, Gabi has worked tirelessly for the Fred Hollows Foundation. This foundation is dedicated towards blindness prevention in more than 26 countries. Gabi Hollows' family also has strong nautical connections: her great-grandfather was a sea captain who established the first slip in Newcastle, New South Wales, while her father was a marine engineer.

"May God bless her and all who sail in her," proclaimed Gabi Hollows before releasing a bottle of champagne against the bow of the Pacific Princess and sparking a spectacular pyro-generated streamer display. Gabi also donated two fine paintings which now hang on the Pacific Princess's forward staircase.

The ship was blessed by Rev Tom Hill, the principal chaplain of the Mission to Seafarers in NSW. Other speakers at the event included NSW Tourism Minister Sandra Nori and P&O Cruises Australia Chairman Richard Hein.

The Master at the time of the naming ceremony was Captain Christopher Rynd, who worked as a senior officer on the original Pacific Princess, when the 'Love Boat' series was being filmed.

P&O Cruises Australia Managing Director, Gavin Smith, said the christening of Pacific Princess marked the dawn of an exciting new age for Australia's burgeoning cruise industry and coincided with the 70th anniversary of the first P&O cruise to leave from Australia.

P&O House Flag. The quartered flag serves as a proud corporate symbol for a diversified group of some 200 companies operating in over forty countries throughout the world.

Oil by S.D Skillett, 1836. P&O Lines.

The William Fawcet, the first ship chartered by Anderson and Willcox. Oil by W.J.Huggins, P&O Lines.

Propulsion

Pacific Princess is fitted with four Wärtsilä 12V32LNE diesel electric engines which produce 13,500 kW at 720 rpm. They are resiliently mounted to reduce vibration and operate on heavy fuel oil. Oil purifiers were supplied by Westfalia and oil/water separators by Sofrance. The comfortable cruising speed is 18 knots and the maximum speed is 21 knots.

The vessel has two Cegelec variable frequency propulsion machines each with a double-winding synchronous motor of 6,750kW at 170 rpm, two six-pulse synchrodrive convertors of 6,750kW and two propulsion transformers of 4,300kVA. GEC Alsthom supplied the four 4.6MW alternators, as well as the 750kW motors for the Brunvoll bow thrusters.

The vessel is fitted with SNACH folding fin anti-roll stabilisers, each of 9.9 square metres. Norske Hydro's green ship waste treatment systems allow waste, including sludge oil, to be incinerated or treated for recycling. The CS3000 Salwico fire protection system has dual-function detectors that are capable of detecting both smoke and heat. The lifeboat system was supplied by Umoe Schat-Harding.

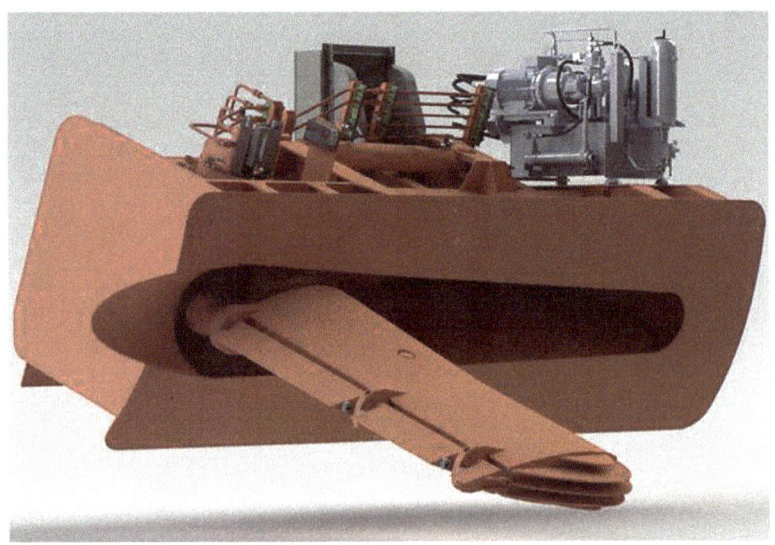

Four of these giant diesel electric engines are installed in the ship.

Mounted under water, the stabilisers are fins projecting from each side of the ship to provide resistance to waves and thus help keep the ship from rolling.

CHAPTER 6

Food, Glorious Food

'Food, Glorious Food, Pork Sausage and Mustard...' But unlike Oliver, if you come to ask for more aboard the Pacific Princess, you're sure to get it With 24-hour room service and an outdoor barbecue complementing the ship's four restaurants, copious amounts of food are an ever-present threat to the waistline.

For breakfast and lunch, the Panorama Buffet is the most popular choice, while, for the more formal evening meal, the main destination is the Club Dining Room.

The two extra tariff restaurants, Sabatini's and the Sterling Steak House Grill offer the passengers an alternative dinner venue. Occupying L-shaped rooms either side of the funnel on deck ten, each has its own private galley and a small terrace overlooking the stern. Sabatini's offers an array of Italian seafood specialties and the decor is Romanesque with eggshell pillars and bas reliefs offset by richly upholstered blue and off-white chairs and matching carpeting.

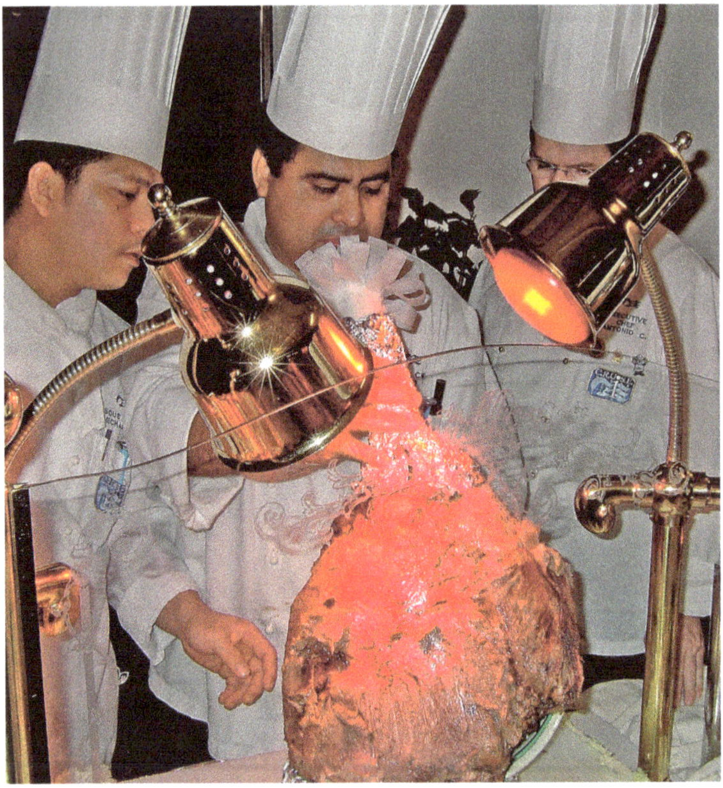

ABOARD PACIFIC PRINCESS | 77

At the buffet, proud chefs show off their food creature creations.

The Sterling's Steakhouse is named after P&O's Lord Sterling who, in 2003 was made Honorary Life President of P&O Cruises. The room features dark panelling with emerald, beige, and brown upholstery. Here, special cuts of beef and side dishes are served in the best of steakhouse traditions.

Behind the scenes, 52 cooks drawn from countries around the world assist the Executive Chef in the preparation of the

DINING AREAS DAILY CONSUMPTION	
Flour 250 Kg	Eggs 3600
Milk 500 litres	Rice 100 Kg
Sugar 50 Kg	Tea Bags 1000
Bacon 65 Kg	Butter 90 Kg
Cheeses 70 Kg	Turkey 75 Kg
Beef 180 Kg	Seafood 130 Kg
Lamb 50 Kg	Lettuce 150 Kg
Chicken 170 Kg	Tomatoes 120 Kg
Carrots 70 Kg	Watermelons 80 Kg
Potatoes 250 Kg	Melons 140 Kg
Pineapples 100 Kg	Wine 280 Bottles
Breadsticks 1500	Beers 750 Cans and Bottles

meals. On a typical cruise you might find that from France and the Philippines come three sous chefs, from Italy, the chief pastry cook, and from Mexico the chief butcher, while the chief baker is from the Philippines.

To serve it all, the Maitre d' Hotel is assisted by a team of 68 waiters. While many come from the Philippines, the staff also comes from countries as far afield as Poland, Romania, Thailand, Slovakia and Portugal.

After feeding so many, washing-up is quite a job. Pot washing, dishes and cleaning is tackled by a crew of eighteen from India. Add in a provisions master, assistant bakers, butchers, storekeepers and gallery helpers and the total number of food service personnel reaches 154.

On a typical ten-day cruise, approximately 40 tons of food is consumed. The daily shopping list is formidable. And so, you can see why, aboard the Pacific Princess, you will never go hungry, here is a list of the main items consumed each day in the dining areas.

PACIFIC PRINCESS RECIPES

As Demonstrated Aboard

Fettuccine Alfredo

To serve ● ● ● ●

Ingredients

• 500 gr fettuccine • 3 cups heavy cream • 100 gr cooked ham cut into strips • 50 gr onions • 50 gr butter • chopped parsley • 50gr grated parmesan cheese • salt, pepper, and nutmeg

Preparation

Melt the butter into a frying pan, add the onions and stir until golden brown. Add the turkey and the ham strips and stir for five minutes. Add the heavy cream, salt, pepper and nutmeg. Stir until a creamy sauce develops. Add the cooked pasta into the sauce and stir, add the grated parmesan into the pasta. Place the mixture onto a dish and decorate with the chopped parsley.

Tomato Sauce

To serve ● ● ● ● ● ●

Ingredients

• 1.5 kg of tomatoes, peeled, seeded and chopped • 4 basil leaves • 2 tablespoons of chopped onion • 2 tablespoons of olive oil • ½ medium size carrot (whole) • ½ medium size celery (whole) • 2 garlic cloves, chopped • ½ teaspoon of sugar • Salt and freshly ground black pepper to taste

Preparation

Pour the olive oil in a skillet on medium heat. Add the ions and sauté until translucent; add the garlic, the tomatoes, the carrot and celery (this will help to remove excessive tartness). Simmer on medium to low heat for about twenty minutes, stirring occasionally until the tomatoes are cooked and form a consistent sauce. Add the basil leaves towards the end of the cooking time.

Scampi Fra' Diavolo

To serve ● ● ● ●

Ingredients

• 1 kg scampi • 3 cups tomato sauce • 1 cup flour • 1 teaspoon parsley finely chopped • ½ cup of olive oil • 2 garlic cloves, finely chopped • 1 teaspoon of crushed red chilli peppers • 50 gr butter • 1 jigger of brandy • salt and pepper to taste

Preparation

Lightly coat the scampi with flour seasoned with salt. Put a skillet on medium heat and add the olive oil. When hot, sauté the garlic until translucent and add the crushed chilli pepper. Add the shrimps and allow to cook for a minute. Flame with brandy, letting it evaporate and add the tomato sauce. Leave the shrimps to simmer for another minute, add the butter for thickening and sprinkle with parsley before serving.

Tiramisu

To serve ● ● ● ● ● ● ● ● ● ●

Ingredients

• 8 egg yolks • 8 egg whites • 150 gr refined sugar • 100 g strong espresso coffee with no sugar added • 60 ml sweet Marsala wine, or Kalua • 20 Lady Finger sponge biscuits • 500g mascarpone cheese • 2 tablespoons cacao powder

Preparation

1. Beat the egg yolks with half the sugar in a cooking bowl.
2. In a separate bowl, beat the egg whites until stiff and form into peaks.
3. Mix mascarpone cheese, Marsala Wine and the remaining sugar with the egg yolks. Then whisk slowly.
4. Gently fold the egg whites into the mixture.
5. In individual champagne saucers, place two sponge biscuits dipped in espresso coffee.
6. Using a spoon, dress the mascarpone cheese mixture on top, up to the rim of each glass.
7. Dust with cacao powder.
8. Refrigerate for two hours before serving.

CHAPTER 7

Ports of Call

The varied itinerary of the Pacific Princess has taken her from the ice floes of Alaska to the white sands of the South Pacific. Whether she is in Asia, India or East Africa, Tahiti or Hawaii, China or the South Pacific, due to her low draft, Pacific Princess can explore many exotic ports of call where other ships with deeper drafts cannot venture.

Downunder, she visits South Pacific islands, the Australian Great Barrier Reef, Tasmania, New Zealand and New Caledonia.

Pacific Princess has chalked up a number of notable firsts. She was the first cruise ship ever to visit the idyllic hideaway of the tiny coral atoll of Wala in Vanuatu. Se was also one of the first to call at Vanuatu's jungle-clad Pentecost Island. Here daredevil islanders re-enact for passengers the awesome ancient ritual of 'naghol', or vine jumping. The jumpers use liana vines tied to their ankles to leap towards the ground from high towers. This ancient custom caught the eye of some New Zealanders who decided to swap the vines for a rope of rubber. Thus, the international sport of bungy jumping was born.

The captain can control the ship from the wing of the bridge to bring it safely alongside a wharf.

In some places there is insufficient depth of water to allow the ship to dock, so the shops lifeboats are used to take passengers ashore.

Another exotic port of the cruise itinerary is the sleepy outpost of Loganville on Vanuatu's largest island, Espiritu Santo. This was a major US base during World War 2 and featured in James Michener's famous novel *'Tales of the South Pacific'* which was subsequently made into the Oscar Hammerstein's musical, *'South Pacific'*.

The impact of the first arrival of a cruise ship on a community is quite spectacular to witness. For example, the Pacific Princess was the first cruise ship to visit Poum, which is tucked away deep in the South Pacific, just north of the Tropic of Capricorn. It is a part of New Caledonia, which, with its splendid beaches and coral waters, has a long history of tourism. The French were the first. They popped by in 1768 but by 1853 they liked it so much they decided to colonise the place. Thus, New Caledonia acquired a capital, which soon sported boulangeries, pharmacies, restaurants and a Club Med. They called it Noumea.

But even by the beginning of the third millennium, in the village of Poum, 450 kilometres away on the northern most end of Grand Terre Island, all the activity down the south end of the island had gone largely unnoticed. Here some 1696 Melanesians carried on cattle rearing and fishing in their traditional way. That was not to say they had not moved with the times. After all, they worked with the French in an open cut nickel mining operation to remove the top of the hills backing their village, drank Coca Cola and new the name of every player in the Rugby World Cup.

 Nevertheless, the village leaders decided that they had been missing out on their share of the tourism spoils. A deal was struck with P&O Lines, financial support and encouragement from Mother France was obtained and the community went into action. In the local Kanak language Poum means "smoke" and the villagers decided it would be good fun to make some. In the weeks before the Pacific

Princess was to make her maiden arrival, the Melanesians set out from their sturdy corrugated tin-roofed homes to build a new village of native grass huts. This was complete with Ceremonial Square, elaborately carved and coloured totem poles, beer hut and trinket stands. Monuments were erected, standing almost as tall and proud as the spectacularly colourful group of individual toilet huts built beside the Catholic Church. The mobile phone transmitting tower was discretely tucked behind a convenient high stand of palms. Now Poum was really looking good!

In the early morning sunshine of a Saturday morning in November 2003, the Pacific Princess sailed into the mirrored waters of the bay to become Poum's first regular customer. The villagers changed out of their jeans and t-shirts, donned grass skirts and body paint, parked their cars out of sight behind the new tourist village and tried their hand out at their first ceremonial greeting gig. They were very colourful. They made the 640 strong contingent of mostly Australian passengers look positively dowdy. And that in itself was no mean achievement. Good natured speeches were made, and the village chief ceremonially exchanged gifts with Pacific Princess Captain Graham Goodway. There was much singing and native dancing.

Those of the local community not actively participating in the welcoming celebrations looked on in amusement from the deepest shadows of a stand of mango trees. Listening to the tribal singing and watching the grass skirts swirl, they broke into broad smiles. They had never seen their mates dressed like that before! The visits of the Pacific Princess became a cause for celebration; it also improved the life and economy of the village and brought enjoyment to the passengers.

Where ever the Pacific Princess roams, whether she is calling at a favourite destination, or opening up some entire new area of tourism, the experience for the passengers is always memorable. But no matter how good the day ashore, returning passengers find nothing more beautiful or welcoming than their first sight of Pacific Princess in a peaceful anchorage. There she sits, shimmering-white amidst blue sea and sky, patiently awaiting her passengers' return.

When cruising aboard such a fine ship, the destinations may be great, but it is the experience of the actual journey that is the best.

TYPICAL NATIONALITIES LIST
Officers and crew on board Pacific Princess

Austria	1	Nepal	3
Australia	29	New Zealand	3
Canada	10	Philippines	169
Switzerland	1	Poland	10
Croatia	5	Portugal	2
Finland	3	Romania	16
Great Britain	22	Thailand	17
Hungary	3	Ukraine	1
Eire	1	United States	4
India	25	South Africa	6
Italy	16		
Mexico	15	**Total people**	**362**

CHAPTER 8

Pieces of Eight

Arr – 'arr me hearties! As every good pirate would know, pieces of eight are pure gold and in this chapter we offer you some little nuggets of nautical knowledge that will make you into a sea-seasoned, genuine sea salt with which you can astound your fellow ship lovers.

The Weighty Issue of Tons

First off, let's understand that gross tonnage is all about the volume inside of a ship and not it's actual weight. The gross tonnage of Oasis of the Seas is 225,282.

Her displacement, that's the actual mass of the vessel, is estimated at approximately 100,000 metric tons (110,000 short tons). This is slightly less than that of an American Nimitz-class aircraft carrier.

The difference between 'ton' and 'tonne' is that a 'ton' is a British and American measure, while a 'tonne' is a metric measure.

A 'tonne' is equal to 1,000 kg. In the US it may be referred to as a metric ton.

Cruising New Caledonia's Woodin Canal.

The British ton, which is also used in other countries that use the Imperial system of weights and measures, is equal to 2,240 pounds or 1,016.047 kg. It is sometimes referred to as the 'long ton', 'weight ton' or 'gross ton'

The North American ton, which is only used in the United States and Canada, is equal to 2,000 pounds or 907.1847 kg. It is sometimes referred to as the 'short ton' or 'net ton'.

The difference dates from the 19th century when the British adapted the avoirdupois system to create the more easily convertible Imperial system. The Americans continued to use the old avoirdupois units. This also explains why there are differences between other British and American measures, most notably pints and gallons – and why the English measure their body weight in stone while the Americans use pounds. Maybe it was all a bid by the English to make them feel they weigh less!

These different measures have specific applications in particular fields of industry, commerce or shipping. So, as we are dealing here with ships, the term gross tonnage, abbreviated as G.T. is an index related to a ship's overall internal volume. So, Gross tonnage is different from gross register tonnage. But neither gross tonnage nor gross register tonnage is a measure of the ship's displacement (mass) and should not be confused with terms such as deadweight tonnage or displacement.

Gross tonnage, along with net tonnage, was adopted by the International Maritime Organization in 1969, and came into force on July 18, 1982. These two measurements replaced gross register tonnage (GRT) and net register tonnage (NRT).

Gross tonnage is calculated not by the weight of the ship but is based on the molded volume of all enclosed spaces of the ship. This is used to determine things such as a ship's manning regulations, safety rules, registration fees, and port dues. The older gross register tonnage was a measure of the volume of only certain enclosed spaces on the ship.

So, there you have it. Got it? Phew. Glad we now have that one all cleared up!

Who Was That? Who Was That!

Aboard ship you will notice a variety of officers' uniform insignias. Worn on the sleeve of a jacket or, in tropical waters, on a shirt as an epaulette, the color and the number of stripes tells you just who's who in the zoo.

First check the color of the space between the stripes. If it is white, it signifies that it is a member of the hotel management. If it is purple, you have just spotted an engineer or electrician. Red is a color you hope only to meet socially. It signifies medical. Green is used to indicate communications, or what used to be called radio officers. It's a lot more significant than simple radio these days. Watch out if its bronze, as that means the ship's police or security. And if there is no color at all between the stripes, then that

The stripes of the deck officers aboard Pacific Princess. Badge Insignias (from the top):

The Captain – in command.

Staff Captain, the second in command and head of the deck department.

Senior First Officer and Statutory Safety Officer.

First Officer.

Second Officer.

Third Officer.

Pictured on the bridge is Captain Graham Goodway who was born in England and grew up in the West Country. He joined P&O as a cadet in 1973 aboard the liner Canberra. He progressed along the traditional route gaining his second mates certificate in four years and his masters another seven years later. He has served on many ships in the P&O fleet.

means the wearer is a bona fide deck officer, in charge of all navigational duties.

Okay! So now we come to the stripes. Obviously, the more the better! Four stripes and you have just met one of the real heavies. It could be the head of the hotel staff, the staff captain, or the chief engineer. If the first of the four stripes is double width, you have just met the captain or the most senior man in that department.

Three stripers are also very senior and indicate First Officers, a doctor or a purser, depending on the color in-between the gold stripes.

Two and a half stripes indicate a Senior Second Officer, two stripes a second officer and one and half stripes a Third Officer.

If there is only one stripe then they are only a cadet, forth officer or petty officer. However, they generally have the advantage of being much younger.

Untying Knots

The knot is a unit of speed to cover one nautical mile in one hour. What is a nautical mile? Well, that is 6080.22 feet. To covert to land miles per hour, you multiply the speed in knots by 1.15.

Why such an odd distance? Well, we are not on land but at sea. One nautical mile is one minute of arc on a free circle of the earth. So that begins to make sense. The world is assumed to have a sphere of radius 3959 miles, and by measuring in minutes of arc, it makes it easy to find the distances along great circles. Doesn't it?

It might sound like taking the long way around, but because the earth is not flat, it is actually the shorter route system used by ships to travel long distances. Simple, isn't it?

Measuring Up

The measurement of a ship's length is commonly taken as the length overall (LOA), or the length between perpendiculars (LBP) at the water line. The depth is measured from the keel to the upper continuous deck.

The draft is measured from the keel to the water line of the loaded ship. The beam is the width of the ship. The front of the ship is the bows, the rear is the stern. The starboard side is the right side when facing the front of the ship and the port side is to the left. Now, even on one of the mega sisters, you will never get lost!

Swinging the Ship's Cat

One of the key factors affecting your enjoyment of life aboard a cruise ship is the amount of space around you. This is called the Passenger Space Ratio and is determined by dividing the tonnage by the number of passengers.

A ship with a ratio of 10 or below is likely to leave even the most sociably inclined to feeling a trifle cramped. Ships stating a Passenger Space Ratio of between 10 and 20 are best described as moderate to high density. The Pacific Princess ratio is 44.1 which places her in the very spacious class.

The Coat of Arms

P&O is the abbreviated name for the Peninsular and Oriental Steam Navigation Company and was granted its Coat of arms in its centenary year.

The symbols on the shield represent the four countries linked by the mail services on which the company's foundations were laid. They are: The Lion of England, The Indian Elephant, the Chinese Dragon and the Australian Kangaroo.

The background colours of the shield are the same as those the P&O House flag. These are the Royal colours of Portugal, blue and white and the red and gold of Spain. Their use was granted to the company founders following their support for the legitimist causes in the Civil War in Portugal and Spain in the early 1830s.

The crest is a rising sun, and this has been used by the company since the 1850s. It represents the 'Oriental' part of the company name and was added when the company extended its service to Egypt, where it received its Royal Charter in 1840.

The motto is 'Quis Nos Separabit', which translates as 'Who Shall Separate Us', thus emphasising how ships can bring people together. Originally P&O used 'Quis Separabit, but to avoid clashing with an existing use of the same motto a small change was made when the formal Arms were granted.

BREAKDOWN OF OFFICERS AND CREW ABOARD PACIFIC PRINCESS				
	Officer	Manager / Supervisor	Rating	Total
Accommodations	1	1	38	40
Bars		2	19	21
Buffet Services		2	19	21
Crew Services		2	24	26
General Admin.		4		4
Galley	3	14	55	72
Bureau	18		3	21
Restaurant	2	4	33	39
Cruise Staff	2	4	27	33
Beauty Salon		1	5	6
Casino		1	7	8
Gift Ship		1	4	5
Laundry		1	6	7
Photographers		1	2	3
Deck	8	5	14	27
Electro Tech	6		3	9
Engine	8	7	15	30
Medical	3			3
Total	51	48	263	362

Going Continental

For this book, we have mainly tried to stick with the US system of measuring and weighing things. However, if you are wanting to convert some facts to metric, try the following guide lines:

- 1 meter ≈ 3.26 feet
- 1 kilometer ≈ 0.62 miles
- 1 liter ≈ 0.26 gallons
- 1 kilogram ≈ 2.20 pounds

CHAPTER 9

The Princess Fleet Round-Up

In 2018, with all ships painted white and being repainted to proudly wear the Princess logo on their bows, the fleet numbered eighteen ships with more on the order books. The vessels range in size from under six-hundred to more than a thousand feet. All conform to one of four classes, apart from the small Pacific Princess which, as we have already established, is in a class of its own.

ROYAL CLASS

Royal Princess 2014

Regal Princess 2014

Majestic Princess 2017

Enchanted Princess 2020

Sky Princess 2019

Majestic Princess

These are Royal Caribbean's largest class of ship, although the company has two larger vessels on order for delivery in 2023 and 2025. The Royal ships are built by the renowned Italian shipyard Fincantieri and operate from ports in Asia, Europe and the USA. All the ships in this class have an adult only area. There are slight variations between vessels, but the basic vital statistics are:

- GRT: 142,229 to 14370 GRT
- LENGTH: 1083 feet
- BEAM: 126 feet
- DRAFT: 28 feet
- CRUISE SPEED: 22 knots
- HEIGHT: 217 - 224 feet
- PASSENGERS: 3560 -3660
- CREW: 1346 (Average)
- TOTAL DECKS: 19

GRAND CLASS

Grand Princess 1998 (Refurbished 2016)

Golden Princess 2001

Star Princess 2002

Caribbean Princess

Diamond Princess 2004

Caribbean Princess 2004

Sapphire Princess 2004

Crown Princess 2006

Emerald Princess 2007

Ruby Princess 2008

Enchanted Princess 2020

Smaller than the Grand Class, the first of this type was delivered in 1998. These popular ships form the largest part of the stable in the Princess Fleet. All were built by Fincantieri in Italy except for Diamond and Sapphire Princess which were built in Japan by Mitsubishi. Variations between ships are slight.

- GRT: 107,517 -115,000 GRT
- LENGTH: 949 -951 feet
- BEAM: feet
- DRAFT: 26-29 feet
- CRUISE SPEED: 22.5 knots
- HEIGHT: 186 feet
- PASSENGERS: 2600-2670
- CREW: 1150 (Average)
- TOTAL DECKS: 17

CORAL CLASS

Coral Princess 2002

Island Princess 2002

Built in France by Chantiers de l'Atlantique, these two ships are described as mid-size and can navigate the Panama Canal. Only five ships in the Princess cruises fleet

Coral Princess

are small enough to fit through and open up the route from the Caribbean to Alaska.

- GRT: 91,627 GRT
- LENGTH: 964 feet
- BEAM: 106 feet
- DRAFT: 27 feet
- CRUISE SPEED: 22 knots
- HEIGHT: 204 feet
- PASSENGERS: 1970
- CREW: 900 (Average)
- TOTAL DECKS: 16

SUN CLASS

Sun Princess 1995

Sea Princess 1998

At the time of their launch, the Sun class was amongst the largest cruise ships in the world. The ships appear identical until you examine the wings of the bridge. The Sun has exterior bridge wings while the wings on the Princess are enclosed. Both ships were built by Fincantieri in Italy. Originally the Sea Princess sailed under the P&O flag as the Adonia but rebranded under Princess in 2005.

Sun Princess

- GRT: 77,499 GRT
- LENGTH: 856 feet

- BEAM: 188 feet
- DRAFT: 26.6 feet
- CRUISE SPEED: 22.4 knots
- HEIGHT: 188 feet
- PASSENGERS: 2000
- CREW: 900 (Average)
- TOTAL DECKS: 14

R CLASS

Pacific Princess 1999

If you have read this far into the book, you will know by now that the Pacific Princess is the baby of the fleet and how it offers such a different experience. However, for comparative purposes, here again are her vital statistics:

- GRT: 30,277 GRT
- LENGTH: 593 feet
- BEAM: 83.6 feet
- DRAFT: 19 feet
- CRUISE SPEED: 18 knots
- HEIGHT: 153 feet
- PASSENGERS: 688
- CREW: 373 (Average)
- TOTAL DECKS: 11

Pacific Princess

Acknowledgements

I am truly indebted to Carolyn Pike for her editorial guidance with the original manuscript. Any mistakes which may have crept through the publishing process are despite her help and are all my own work.

For the first edition of this book and my insight into the design process of Pacific Princess, my thanks go to Ron Hughess of McNeece in London who was the design project leader for this beautiful ship. I am also grateful for the help I received from Mark Hilferty, the managing director of McNeece. For the better understanding of life aboard Pacific Princess, my thanks go to Captain Graham Goodway and Passenger Services Director Emilio Mazzi and at the shore offices of P&O Cruises: Gianfranco Verde and Andrew Mevissen. Although the vast majority of the photographs are taken by the author, thanks also go to Princess Cruises for the use of some images.

About the Author

Born in Cornwall, UK, Paul Curtis began contributing photos and articles to newspapers and magazines while still at school.

Before he turned twenty, he took a job aboard a cruise ship as a photographer. For the next six years, Paul mostly worked out of New York City and sailed on ten different liners plying most of the world's cruising grounds.

Towards the end of his sea-going time, he abandoned his camera for the microphone and worked as an entertainment officers aboard the original RMS Queen Mary.

Following the Mary's withdrawal from service, Paul moved to Australia where he entered the business world before returning to writing and establishing a magazine publishing company. Paul also became a frequent radio, tv and press commentator on imaging technology, but has always maintained his lifelong interest in anything that floats.

Paul likes to hear from his readers and can be contacted at paul@paulcurtis.com.au.

By the Same Author

High Tea on the Cunard Queens — A Light-Hearted Look at Life at Sea

The Oasis Sisters (a revised edition of Royal Caribbean's Mega Sisters)

Pacific Princess – The New Love Boat (Now revised as Aboard the Pacific Princess)

A History of Professional Photography in Australia

www.ingramcontent.com/pod-product-compliance
Lightning Source LLC
Chambersburg PA
CBHW040325300426
44112CB00021B/2880